Maximus Poetry

Maximus Poetry

More Of The Best Of Ken Jackson

Ken Jackson

ISBN:	Softcover	978-1-9845-8217-1
	eBook	978-1-9845-8216-4

Print information available on the last page.

Rev. date: 06/02/2020

To order additional copies of this book, contact:
Xlibris
1-888-795-4274
www.Xlibris.com
Orders@Xlibris.com
728753

Contents

I Am Author
a sestina

Wanted a publisher.
Wanted a friend.
Oops made an error.
And made a typo.
Needed a cover.
Snail mail post office.

Went to the post office.
Roselee did publishing.
Want to discover.
Ride through an error.
Roselee's my friend.
Typo, typo, typo.

Post us a typo.
Post, postal post office.
I'm Roselee's boyfriend.
Do some undercover.
Can't go unpublished.
Can't make an error.

Didn't mean to scare her.
Let's use a typewriter
To edit and publish.
We can be friends.
Sent to the principals office.
I'm Roselees lover.

The glove didn't fit.
Machine made an error.
Make me an offer.
To go unpublished.
Under a staple.
Must make amends.

How much to spend.
Heavens above.
Got me some wipe out.
Sent to the post office.
Think I'll just spare her.
Maple Leaf Publishing, Inc.

Even a publisher needs a good friend.
An error is the same as a typo.
Discover the Post Office.

Things Go Sweet

Things will go sweet.
Says Paul and Pete.
Say all the time.
"You will be mine".
All sorts of stuff.
Is well enough.

Swimming in my pool.
I ain't no fool.
That's the way it is.
Here in showbiz.
With the raquetball.
Hit against the wall.

I want to be the president.
Because I am so heavensent.
I can run the United States.
I think it is my fate.
You can call me the boss.
It will be no lose.

Fly above the shining star.
Take me low. Take me far.
See the moon way up high.
Way up there in the sky.
Flying up there in the miles.
Flying up there in the style.

Sweetheart. Sweetheart.
Why must we part.
I'll wait right here.
Don't have no fear.
Don't talk. Don't speak.
Don't look. Don't peek.

Sweet lady. Sweet baby.
Looking good, Looking crazy.
Looking good, Looking nice.
Wonder when. Good size.
Just tell me. Please sell me.
Anytime. Just spell me.

Hey sweety. Hey baby.
Yeah. Yeah. Maybe. Maybe.
Looking for you. Later. Later.
I'll meet you in the elevator.
Can't you see it. Me and you.
You look like not a clue.

Hello
April 1, 2018

Fools. Fool April fool.
I could always use my cool.
Maybe even go to school.
Or I could play some pool.
Flail hail never fail.
Just as big as a whale.
I could go out and sail.
Send it to me through the mail.
Sing sing, Off the wing.
I could feel it tickling.
Go out to the bar and swing.
I could always go missing.
I could fly a kite with string.
With my little dingling

Self Addressed Stamped Envelope
April 2, 2018

Waiting for the mailman.
Waiting for my big package.
Looking for the answer.
Looking for the message.
Could be a magazine.
Could be a big fat check.
Wonder if it's a guitar.
Or a CD of Jeff Beck.
Maybe it's a penpal.
Maybe it's an old old friend.
Seeking out a relative.
Using a stamp to send.
Or pictures for me to send.
And I need a SASE.

Politics
April 3, 2018

Political heart of fate.
And we got to demonstrate.
I guess I got to buy my seat.
I'm not trying to designate
Some day I will be on top.
You got to go before I stop.
And they say that life is free.
Until you go overseas.
Someday I will be on top.
Listen Ma. Listen Pop.
Someday you will see there.
Don't you look.
Don't you stare.
Maybe I will be the President.
Because I am so heavensent.

News
April 4, 2018

I just got the news.
I just got the blues.
When I saw you there.
I am all aware.
I just got the story.
Went to Californy.
I just really love it.
I can live above it.
I am really sorry.
I just pulled a whammy.
I just walk away.
Just what can I say?
I just love to smile.
For just a little while.

Hot Dog
April 5, 2018

I like hot dogs.
With ketchup and mustard.
And I like coffee.
Latte and mocha.
And I like TV,
CDs and stereo.
I try to keep up with the latest.
I got a cell phone.
Gives me junk calls.
I like stereo
AM and FM.
I like to eat.
Eat my hot dog.

Feelings
April 6, 2018

Life is good.
Can't be bad.
Life is great.
Can't be sad.
Living well.
Can't complain.
I am smart
I am sane.
I'm in love.
With myself.
I am cool.
And heartfelt.
When I'm bad.
Makes me sad.

Golf
April 7, 2018

I always like to play golf.
I always like to get a birdie.
I just wanna get a shot.
I don't wanna get a bogey.
A 9-iron is what I need.
To get me a drive.
1st hole. 2nd hole. 3rd hole.
In a golf cart I will arrive.
And I got me a caddy.
And I'll make me a putt.
And I'll be under par.
I'll get to the 18th hole.
Win me. Win me the game.
Meet you at the 19th hole.

Baseball One
April 8, 2018

Spent my Sunday watching TV.
That is what I wanted to see.
I wanted to watch baseball.
That Ryan Braun is ten feet tall.
I try to watch all nine innings.
That seat is hot for the sitting.
Sometimes it goes into the tenth.
Sometimes Brewers do a walk off.
Watch out for broken bats.
Home runs hits out it the stands.
Listen to the songs played out there.
Watching all the baseball stars.
No one should be hurt no more,.
Keep in mind the baseball score.

Credit Card Call
April 9, 2018

Credit card account.
Watch my debt amount.
Working on my plans.
Because I'm the man.
I know how you feel.
Right behind the wheel.
It's a real steal.
It's like a good meal.
And it's all the same.
And I feel the pain.
And I want it framed.
That is what I claim.
I can feel the dirt.
I don't wanna hurt.

Spooky Monday
April 10, 2018

Monday, Monday, Monday.
What the f*ck can I say.
Even though it's Tuesday.
Spiritual invasion.
Looking for the spirit.
Ghosts of what you could call.
Risen from the dead.
Isn't that what I said.
Knocking on the coffin.
Asking for what I need.
Friday the 13th.
Tell me how I could win.
Spooky. Spooky. Spooky.
Monday Monday. Monday.

Lunch Lunch
April 11, 2018

Lunch Lunch
Extended brunch.
Make me a sandwich.
And have an apple.
Because it tastes good.
Just like it should, should.
No problems.
Like Funnocello.
Wait for a day.
Then have another.
All I could say is
'Oh! Brother!'
Loaf of bread.
I'm good for a week.

Serious
April 12, 2018

Serious?
Are you serious?
Are you real?
Are you really serious?
You are what you are.
Close but also far.
You are but a star.
Away with a spar.
Serious?
Are you serious?
You are for real.
Looking for a steal.
Do you make me steal.
Seriously.

Rain
April 13, 2018

Rainy. Rain. Rainy day.
It is total wet.
Water water waterways.
I low much I will bet.
I low many inches?
How many centimeters?
How much water in my shoes?
How much can you say?
Under the weather.
Under the raindrops.
Under my mom.
Under my pop.
Under my neighbors.
Under raindrops.

Hawaii
April 14, 2018

Got a ticket to Hawaii.
Will I ever make it there?
I'll get there by airplane.
I will wear my underwear.
Wonder if I'll ever get there.
People watching my back.
People giving me the stare.
I got my bags packed.
Wonder if I ever make it.
And I really got my doubts.
Fly up there in the air.
I was in the boy scouts.
Just don't stare at me.
I can see the watersports.

MSG
April 15, 2019

Madison Square Garden.
I beg your pardon.
It's where people meet.
To win and defeat.
Madison Square Garden
is where we party.
We have much to drink.
Following a wink.
Madison Square Garden.
Lonely hearted.
We will watch the game.
We will meet our fame.
Madison Square Garden.
Madison Square Garden.

Scary Movies
April 16, 2018

Scary movies.
Starring Boris Karloff.
Scary movies.
Playing Frankenstein.
Scary movies.
Playing Bela Lagosi.
Scary movies.
Playing Dracula.
Scary movies.
Starring Lon Cheney Jr.
Scary movies.
Playing the Wolfman.
Scary movies.
King Kong vs. Godzilla.
Vincent Price I must add.
Peter Cushing is the cad.

Guitar
April 17, 2018

Guitar. Wanna be a star.
Guitar. Wanna make it far.
Guitar. Wanna sing a song.
Guitar Wanna play along.
Guitar. Rock me off to sleep.
Guitar. And my dreams will keep.
Guitar. Plucking on the strings.
Guitar. Everybody sings.
Guitar. Writing me a song.
Guitar. And we'll sing along.
Guitar. With a wooden body.
Guitar. Pleases everybody.
Guitar. Call it rock 'n' roll.
Guitar. Playing from my soul.

Weather
April 18, 2018

Some people are creepy.
Others are crazy.
Some are so weepy.
Just like a daisy.
Some always loving.
Others are hating.
Snow with a shovel.
Pack in the grating.
Wishing the weather
The weather is better.
Raining and snowing.
Put on a sweater.
Snow is so white.
Rain is so right.

Lock Down
April 19, 2018

Watch out for the FBI.
Watch out for the CIA.
They will just get you in trouble.
It depends on what they say.
Don't get into jail.
Or you'll need some bail.
You'll just get behind bars.
You won't have a guitar.
Three hots, a pot and a cot.
And you'll have a private plot.
But the coffee is not bad.
And it's kind of sad.
People die in jail.
Please don't fail.

Radio
April 20, 2018

Listen to the radio.
Listen to so-and-so.
To whoever it may be.
Whoever we would like to see.
If it's just a talk show.
If it's even fast slow.
They are playing CDs.
Vinyl or 8-track.
Even reel-to-reel.
Punk, jazz or rock 'n' roll.
Hip hop or rap.
Even an orchestra.
Anything with a beat.

Replay
April 21, 2018

Replay. Replay.
Replay I say.
Replay wordplay.
No way. No way.
Love to give the news.
Many or the few.
Gotta pay the dues.
Pulling out the fuse.
Replay. Replay.
Replay Today.
Noonday. Foreplay.
Okay. Okay.
Gonna let it go.
With the rain and the snow.

Another Sunday
April 22, 2018

Just another Sunday.
Just one of the week.
Looking for another day.
If I take a peek.
Like a chicken on the road.
To the other side.
Hoping that a car will stop.
Waiting for a ride.
Got my thumb pointing out.
I want to go far.
Got a bag with clothes and socks.
And got my guitar.
Going to California.
Don't say I didn't warn ya.

Laundry Day
April 23, 2018

Laundry day. Laundry day.
What else did I say?
Powdered soap. Powdered soap.
How else can I cope.
Whiter shirt. Whiter shirt.
How much is it worth.
Smelly socks. Smelly socks.
Smell it makes a shock.
Underwear. Underwear.
Enough to make a scare.
Dirty pants. Dirty pants.
Smelling it enhanced.
Bunch of quarters. Bunch of quarters.
What a pickpocket!

Movies
April 24, 2018

Movies? Movies.
Just like in the movies.
Actor? Actors.
Always, always acting.
Artist? Artists.
Wonder who is smarter.
Director? Director.
Controlling the erecting.
Bookie? Bookie.
Wonder who got tookies.
Tickets? Tickets.
Looks just like a sticker.
Sold out? Sold out.
All the tickets sold out.

Titanic
April 25, 2018

It's remarkable.
It's nice.
It's wonderful.
It's great.
What could I do?
We'll see.
We're capable.
To be free.
Unforsaken.
Can't lose.
Unsinkable.
Titanic.
Unbelievable.
The glacier.

Rocking
April 26, 2018

Music really sounds good.
I really have to say.
Gives a good beat on your feet.
Kneel down and pray.
I love stuff from guitar.
Six string, seven or twelve.
If you are sitting at a bar.
Or sitting on a shelf.
Give it to Bass and Drum.
Or you're booked in a band.
You could rock 'n' roll 'n' rock.
Kicking up the sand.
Remember me while making sound.
I'll be your favorite fan.

Bluegrass
April 27, 2018

Listen to that bluegrass.
With the banjo going fast.
Happy songs and sad songs.
Wishes that will last.
Wonder what will happen?
If there was a trend.
Towards bluegrass music.
Where the message sends.
With the harmonica,
banjo and guitar.
With the bluegrass bands.
Last ones in the bar.
Is it worth a drink?
Just to be a star.

Baseball Two
April 28, 2018

Baseball is a serious business.
You have to keep on track of the scores.
You gotta know right from wrong.
You gotta know what's in store.
You gotta steal a base, oh, yeah!
Ir's really not that bad.
It's not like you're breaking the law.
But it really makes the pitcher sad.
When you hit the ball over the fence.
It's called a homer (home run).
It get hotty-hot-hot-hot!
It gets hot in the sun.
And it lasts 9 innings.
And they count the runs.

April 2019

Guess
April 1, 2019

Get on the seat.
Get on the ride.
Put on the boots.
Get on the side.
Get on the front.
Get on the back.
Get on the wheel.
Grab on my sack.
Doing a wheelie.
Pull on the wheel.
Girl on the back now.
Doing a steel.
Doing a psyche.
On motorcyle.

Stamp
April 2, 2019

Waiting for something.
Something to happen.
Happening here now.
Now tree to sappen.
Sappening sunshine.
Sun shining good tan.
Tan at the station.
Station-to-station.
Stationing something.
Something to happen.
Happening here now.
Now tree to sappen.
Sappening somewhere.
Somewhere and stamping.

Baseball Three
April 3, 2019

Baseball is the game.
Not always the same.
Got the Hall Of Fame.
Picture I could frame.
Chop out at the bat.
Read out at the stat.
Dogs and the cat.
That's where I did sat.
Then I hit the ball.
Hope that I don't fall.
Watch the pitcher stall.
And my brother Paul.
Ball bounced off the wall.
And he's six feet tall.

Journey
April 4, 2019

Going on a journey.
Going on a trip.
Listening to people.
It just makes me sick.
Where are we going?
Wonder where it ends.
Going on forever.
That's the way it goes.
Tell me what will happen.
Wonder what will be.
Where will we go?
Wonder what we see.
Going on forever.
What have we seen.

Sing
April 5, 2019

Sing praise sing.
Sing, sing, sing.
Make noise. Make noise.
Make news noise.
Noise news noise.
Neat noise news.
Na, na, na.
No. no. no.
Ned Nate None.
News nun is neat.
Neato news.
News noise sing.
Sing, sing, sing.
Sing song sing.

DejaVu
April 6, 2019

What you see is what you get.
All because my heart set.
See where we walk the beat.
And that I could find my seat.
That is where I found my love.
That is where I take a shove.
Wonder how I found my way.
And I don't have much to say.
Looking at my point of view.
And I got a nary clue.
Looking over up and down.
And I didn't make a sound.
Someday I will find a way.
And I won't have much to say.

Coffee
April 7, 2019

Coffee w/ a friend.
Caffeine and we will send.
Dark roast tastes so good.
Tastes good like it should.
Why it tastes that way.
Taste good, that's the what I say.
It got that color black.
And it got that pack/smack.
Like it got that taste.
Don't let it go to waste.
I look at it face-to-face.
I get up and wanna pace.
Coffee makes me kind of high.
Enough to make me ask why.

Newspaper
April 8, 2019

I read the newspaper.
And it's a good read.
It is my caper.
The news I will read.
It's like a vapor.
And I take the lead.
And I sow the seed.
And I see the need.
I write the newspaper.
And it's a good lead.
It is my caper.
And I'll take the lead.
Paper, paper, paper.
Paper, paper, paper.

Mailman
April 9, 2019

Say hello to the mailman.
He does a real good job.
He delivers the packages.
He ain't no slob.
He don't drink whiskey.
He don't drink wine.
He reads the zip code.
We read the sign.
You put on a stamp.
He deliver the check.
If it's the wrong address
He say "What the heck!"
He drives away.
He don't get no wreck.

Question?
April 10, 2019

What will happen to me?
What we ever to see?
What will happen tonight?
When we'll ever to fight?
Will I ever wake up?
What we drink from a cup?
What we put on the table?
When we put on the cable?
When we sit on the couch?
Where did I get this slouch?
Where did we put my shoes?
I haven't got a clue?
Answer to the question?
What is the suggestion?

Peeker
April 11, 2019

Look at it this way.
Look at it that way.
Look at the problem.
What can I say?
Have a solution.
Look for an answer.
It makes me wonder.
Look for a solution.
Give me a good line.
We play anything.
It makes me wonder.
I'm a good lover.
I want a seeker.
I am a peeker.

Bernie Sanders Gets My Vote
April 12, 2019

Hail! Hail! Bernie Sanders!
I'm just trying to understand ya'.
I know you're a politician.
And it gets people a-wishing.
I know that you got a low score.
And you got my noggin sore.
But I really like your style.
Prez you will be in a while.
Bernie will be in my vote.
And you'll get it note for note.
I hope you will like my poem.
And it will get you a-knowing.
And you'll get our sentiments.
Bernie Sanders for President.

The Sun
April 14, 2019

Weekends are for fun.
You are number one.
I love you a ton.
I really love the sun.
I really love you today.
I really love to say.
Any. Anyway.
Love me any day.
Go out to the sea.
Go out you and me.
Funny pay a fee.
And it isn't free.
Oh my. Oh my God.
OMG.

Notre Dame
April 15, 2019

My regards to Notre Dame.
It was great to some.
Really went to heart.
And a lot of art.
Historical monument.
Really was heaven sent.
800 years to the day.
What can I do? What can I say?
It was great to you and me.
I am not a politician.
It was where I got cognition.
Memory will be great.
Heaven will be 'oh' great.

Friends
April 16, 2019

Seeking restoration.
Sorry for your patience.
Looking for my future.
Hoping it's mature.
Going to a meeting.
Looking for deleting.
Looking for an answer.
Trying to beat cancer.
Looking for a feeling.
Staring at the ceiling.
Checking on my mail.
Looking to set sail.
Looking for a friend.
I guess it's the end.

Record
April 17, 2019

Looking out the window.
Wonder where we go.
Asking for an answer.
Put me out to pasture.
Loving every minute.
Going past my limit.
Loving every second.
Going out to Mecca.
Driving to a wrecka.
Listen to a record.
Loving every second.
Listen to the music.
Pounding every second.
Pounding, Pounding. Pounding.

I Didn't Say
April 18, 2019

Didn't say "Yes".
Didn't say "No".
I think of "Stop".
I wanna "Go".
What I "say".
Is what I "Mean".
I dress up.
I made the scene.
I wanna "screw".
If I get some luck.
Just what I did.
It really sucks.
I answered "Yes".
Didn't say "No".

Class
April 19, 2019

Class. Class. Class.
I certainly got class.
I just went alas.
Class. Class. Class.
Whip. Whip. Whip.
Don't mean to give lip.
Sip. Sip. Sip.
Hip. Hip. Hip.
Look. Look. Look.
See what I just took.
Wrote me a good book.
Cook. Cook. Cook.
Got me on a hook.
See what I fortook.

Comfort
April 20, 2019

Sitting in the cabin.
All nice, all warm.
Looking at the cat and
looking at the farm.
Taking it easy.
Every wonderful way.
Every ways and means.
What more can I say?
Sitting back in my chair.
Feeling pretty good.
Feeling pretty comfortable.
Just like I should.
No time to lose.
Gotta snooze.

Cat
April 21, 2019

Hey Cat. Kitty cat.
Where did you go?
I thought I saw you with
missus so-and-so.
And I saw you making
all that noise.
And I saw you hanging
out with the boys.
And I saw you making
all that mess.
You look like you came from
the wild, wild west.
Take you in for a refund.
Sitting in the hot sun.

Motorcycle
April 22, 2019

Traffic. Just a lot of cars.
Traffic. Just a lot of stars.
Traffic. Taking off to Mars.
Traffic. Traffic.
Wheelies. Pull back the steer.
Engines. Get rid of fear.
Chrome. Shine up the gear.
Motorcycle.
Skids put on the brakes.
Pull out for goodness sake.
Rubber. That is the make.
Weather. Aware.
Burn out on my motorcycle.
Faster that a bicycle.

I Want It All
April 23, 2019

People say they want it all.
They're acting like they're 10 feet tall.
They don't act like they want to say.
They don't exactly want to stay.
Maybe they need a cup of joe.
And they really want to go.
But they don't know what they need.
But they don't know what to eat.
But they know just what to take.'
"Make up your minds for goodness sake."
What they need is a little wit.
And to watch just where they sit.
Just remember what you say.
Now just gotta get away.

Now
April 24, 2019

Looking in the past.
Going to the future.
Anything for the presence.
Giving for the now.
Seeing one another.
Looking in your eyes.
Seeing for each other.
Going for that size.
Whipping for each other.
Loving anyway.
Friday any other.
Handing out the lies.
Friday is so wise.
Friday is for lies.

Las Vegas
April 25, 2019

Las Vegas is where it's at.
That is where you wear your hat.
Money. Money. Win some money.
That is where you go to honey.
Clink. Clink, Clink. In the sink.
Where you have to make a wink.
Try to win a lot of coins.
And it's close to Cali torn.
That is where the slot machine.
Got you going like a fiend.
Also play some 21.
And you also pack a gun.
And you're also counting cards.
Playing there can be so hard.

Newspaper Two
April 26, 2019

I saw a newspaper story about me.
It's something that read for free.
It has a lot of stuff about me.
It is something you have to see.
It makes me wonder all about me.
It is more than I could say.
Like I said It's all about me.
And you don't need to pay.
So if you want to find about me.
You just turn it to the page.
Then you'll find all about me.
And you don't need to pay a wage.
So read the story all about me.
And please read every page.

What To Eat
April 27, 2019

Some things I like to eat.
Are veggies and some meat.
Are burgers and some fries.
And pizza is so wise.
Also coffee I go out.
I can lit it in my mouth.
Cheesy. Cheesy. I like cheese.
Hand me some Lasagne please.
Hot dogs cooked upon the grill.
A Big Mac really gets my fill.
Don't forget burritos please.
Mustard really gets my squeeze.
That is what I like to eat.
That is where I get my meat.

Baseball Four
April 28, 2019

I like watching baseball.
Except when they get beaned.
Feel like a baseball.
Stitching is so mean.
Hit it with a bat.
Flying over the fence.
Reminds me of campground.
Living in a tent.
Walking in a stadium.
Going to my seat.
Cheering for the players.
Looking for the sweep.
Watching for the home run.
It is just so sweet.

Bank
April 29, 2019

I like going to the bank.
Like my ship it sank.
And I cheek money out.
And I get an amount.
Signing a receipt.
Really is a feat.
I don't get a lot.
Just to get me hot
The teller always smiles.
They got me on a file.
Hope they don't get robbed.
By some drunken slob.
But what they got.
Comes into my plot.

Morning Blues
April 30, 2019

Oh. I get up in the morning.
And I got the blues.
Then I eat breakfast.
Gotta pay my dues.
I puff my pillow.
And then I go.
Put on my shoes.
Like so-and-so.
I eat breakfast.
And brush my teeth.
Put on my glasses.
So I could see.
Look out the window.
If I please.

November 2019
PANTOUMS

Power Player
November 1, 2019

One day I was sayin'
Everyone was prayin'
Going to the supermarket.
And I knew just where to park it.

Dragging on my great big suitcase.
Looking for that dogman f*uckface.
Sitting on my great big wallet.
Going to that School LaFollette.

Wishing that I had a bonnet.
I just want to get on it.
Wonder if I get to heaven.
And I know 6 foot 7.

I am really, really lonely.
I am also, also only.
Finding out is really spiritual.
And my soul, soul is peritial.

Finding out I'm really wild.
Looking in my mirror and smile.
Now I got to go to bed.
Thinking of just what I said.

Clint Eastwood
November 2, 2019

Watching Clint Eastwood doing his stuff.
Can't you just tell him we had enough.
Waiting for him to do his thing.
Listening, listening to hear him sing.

He is the greatest, greatest around.
And when he sings, can't hear a sound.
Waiting just waiting for him on Christmas.
Time comes around to do a census.

Clint Eastwood, he is always the man.
Everyone sits while he just stands.
And he just surely has lots of fans.
I use to draw him as a big man.

And he is working all of the time.
Wouldn't you know it. That it all rhymes.
He shoots his gun at the big sign.
And he just nicks all just so fine.

And I just can't, can't quite complain.
And it just happens all in the same.
But he is really just a good friend.
All I could say is this is the end.

Funny Money
November 3, 2019

Funny, money, honey.
Looking very sunny.
Funny, funny, funny.
Money, money, money.

Honey, honey, honey.
Money, money, money.
Looking very sunny.
Funny, funny, funny.

Looking very sunny.
Funny, funny, funny.
Looking at my tummy.
Money, money, money.

Money, money, money.
Looking at my money.
Funny, funny, funny.
Money, money, money.

Funny, funny, funny.
Looking very sunny.
Funny, funny, funny.
Money, money, money.

Send
November 4, 2019

Sinking Willowbee
Hearts do trend
Wondering how come
When we send

Wuthering winds
Totally trend
Firing firecrackers
Suddenly send

Horrible hooky hustle
Totally fried.
Looking into you
On the best side.

Firing firecrackers
Sending into
Looking at the way
Haven't a clue

What will happen if
The blathering half wit
And the way we sit
That we will send

My Radio
November 5, 2019

Me and my radio.
Ain't that the way to go.
Please don't say it ain't so.
Me and my radio.

I guess it's the season.
I am a man of reason.
There's no way of pleasing.
Me and my radio.

Me and my radio.
Looking for the green and gold.
It's just so wonderful.
Me and my radio.

Looking for a better way.
Looking for a better day.
Looking for some better pay.
Me and my radio.

Me and my radio.
Ain't that the way to go.
Please don't say it ain't so.
Me and my radio.

Black Light Bulb
November 6, 2019

Fresh air
Fresh will
Fresh mountain lion
Fresh kill

Fresh love
Fresh hate
Fresh fish
I ate

Fresh sun
Fresh moon
Fresh stars
So soon

Fresh monkey
Fresh lune
Fresh giraffe
Fresh zoo

Fresh pizza
Fresh cheese
Fresh fight
in ease

Conquistador Elephants
November 7, 2019

Thoughts of delusion
going though my head.
Conquistador elephants.
That's what what she said.

Thinking of suicide.
Going through my head.
Conquistador elephants.
That's what she said.

So what if I got your
name wrong I said.
Conquistador elephants.
That's what she said.

Maybe its on your
voicemail instead.
Conquistador elephants.
That's what she said.

I saw you lying
On top of your bed.
Conquistador elephants.
That's what she said.

Cleaning Daze
November 8, 2019

Loving, living
Always forgiving
Sleeping, lying
Even close to dying

Cleaning, sweeping
Always weeping
Weeping, crying
See birds-a-flying

Praying, needing
Just watch him pleading
Hating, killing
Oh, so willing

Sliding hiding
Always fighting
Sweating, fretting
I am-a-spitting.

Binoculars looking
I am-a-spooking
Sleeping, snoring
The rains-a-pouring

Green Bay Blues
November 9, 2019

Sweet chili beans
Are so good
Tastes the same
like they should

Sweet burritos
Are so bad
Makes me feel
Oh so sad

Green Bay Packers
Are so good
They play so good
Like they should

Chicago Bears
Are so bad
Let me tell you
They been had

Nobody knows
How much fun
There is when
When the season is done

Sunday Marbles
November 10, 2019

Sunday, Sunday is a fun day.
Train goes down the track.
Sunday. Monday. Tuesday. Wednesday.
Time to hit the sack.

Stupid people in the steeple.
Time to look so black.
It's so sunny. It's so funny.
Looking at the plaque.

On the ground shooting marbles.
Feeling oh so blue.
Oh so weirdy. Got a perie.
That's what we must do.

Later on. Grow so fond.
Loving everyday.
Even when it grows so dark.
And I hear you say:

"Sunday, Sunday is a fun day.
Train goes down the tracks.
Sunday. Monday. Tuesday, Wednesday.
Time to hit the sack."

Outer Space
November 11, 2019

What would happen if?
If I did a riff.
On my guitar.
Playing so-and-so.

Maybe I will play.
Maybe I will say.
Moving up in class.
Sassy, sassy, sass.

I'm in outer space.
And I'm in face-to-face.
With another jerk.
And a desk clerk.

I go to work.
As a soda jerk.
I'm in outer space.
And I'm face-to-face.

And all the coins clink.
Haven't slept a wink.
And I'm face-to-face.
In outer space.

It's Cold Today
November 12, 2019

It's cold today.
The kids are out to play.
Anyway.
What have you got to say.

There's snow outside.
It's on the ground.
There are snowflakes.
Going past the speed of sound.

It's freezing out.
There's footprints on the ground.
It's very cold.
And snow piled up around.

Kids playing out.
Building big snowforts.
Throwing snowballs.
At the old folks lounge.

The snow is deep.
Right up to knees.
It makes me sleep.
Temperature makes me sneeze.

Tuna
November 13, 2019

I am a slam bam man.
I do what I can.
With a fixer upper.
And I do what I can.

Living in a nightmare.
I'm a mighty man.
Really made a line.
With my Crayola crayon.

Maybe if I'm better.
Maybe if I'm a man.
And I'll make a line.
Right across the sand.

Open a tuna can.
That is what I plan.
I am just a fan.
Of my tuna man.

Looking at Google Chrome.
That is on the phone.
Leave me all alone.
Make my way back home.

Come Home Late
November 14, 2019

Looking out for my
S. O. B.
Looking out for
You and me

Waiting here
Here in line
Standing there
Next to the sign

Pathetic losers
Standing around
Just waiting around
The lost and found

Hope I don't
Catch the mumps
And I know
It ain't no fun

So I'll just
Stand here and wait
Hope I don't
Come home late

Fishing Trip
November 15, 2019

Pull out your worm.
Put it on the hook.
Cast out the line.
The bobber sank.

The fish took hold.
He took the line.
The water splashed.
Shook all the time.

The pole then bent.
Pulled in the fish.
Looked like a bass.
Looked like a dish.

I pulled in four.
Like five or six.
A couple perch.
Like five or six.

A Northern Pike.
Or even a Musky.
36 inches.
It is so husky.

Don't
November 16, 2019

Don't get too excited.
Don't get too into it.
Don't get too romantic.
Don't get too...

Don't get too athletic.
Don't get to the little girl.
Horses gallop to the beat.
Don't go to the world.

What will happen if I stay?
What will happen if I go?
Say something happy to the place.
Say something that know.

Publish something in the end.
Just drop the beat.
Headache, headache, headache.
My heart's for you girl.

Don't get too excited.
Don't get into it.
Don't get too romantic.
Don't get too...

Exercises
November 17, 2019

Exercises.
Exercises are important to you.
Exercises.
Exercises to the fortunate few.

Exercises.
Exercises can get you in shape.
Exercises.
Exercises can make it grape.

Exercises.
Exercises can make you feel good.
Exercises.
Exercises are misunderstood

Exercises.
Exercises can make you so strong.
Exercises.
Exercises are like a great a great song.

Exercises.
Exercises can control how you spend.
Exercises.
Exercises arc good to the soul.

Hey Smoothie
November 18, 2019

Hey! Smoothie!
Eating up the weather.
Big problem.
Almost as light as a feather.

Hey! There!
What can we see?
Just thinking about
All the birds and the bees.

Hey! Buddy!
Thinking kid of loose.
Looking a place
For all the ducks and the geese.

Hey! Stinker!
Boy, you really stink.
You have to face it, boy.
You're a big nerdy fink.

Hey! Hey! Momma!
I could be your man.
Anyway you see it.
I'll be your fan.

Please
November 19, 2019

Please see her
A passenger ride.
Lets fear her.
Let's get inside.

Big mighty train
going down the tracks.
Reading my notebook.
Let's sell crack.

If you think I'm looking busy.
You can see how far I go.
Wondering how far I got.
And I told you so.

And I need a typewriter.
To get over the hills.
I'm busy feeling bad.
Knock it back with pills.

If you really need a ride.
Baby come inside.
The man inside really lied.
And the baby cried.

Tit For Tat
November 20, 2019

What a catch
Gone so bad
Baseball mitt
Like I been had

And I wonder
What will happen
Tire swing
Trees will sappen

Please don't worry
In God we trust
Silver coins
Turn to rust

Over upside
Upside down
Ninety degrees
Lost and found

I'm in love
W/ close neighbor
Neighbor first
Then close second

Me So Horny
November 21, 2019

Me so horny.
Way you gotta do it.
Doing a trick.
And you gotta fool it.

Me so horny.
What you gotta do.
Trying to score.
And you make the fool.

Me so horny.
Me, I gotta cry.
Way it's gotta be.
And I wonder why.

Me so horny.
And you talking sex.
And it's as big as
Tyrinasauras Rex.

Me so horny.
And it's all over.
I feel lucky as a
four leaf clover.

Loud Music
November 22, 2019

Loud music
That's what I like
Ride on
my motorbike

Loud music
Party down
Going down
the laser sword

Loud music
Plug my ears
Pretty loud
Have no fear

Loud music
Rock 'n' roll
With that jazz
Lot of soul

Loud of music
Plain amusing
Beatles music
And we're cruising

Day In November
November 23, 2019

Day in November,
Feels pretty loose.
Losing my hair.
Loose as a goose.

Day in November.
Feeling so tight.
Nights have come and gone.
It's out of sight.

Day in November.
Who is it now?
What is the snow?
Where is the plow?

Day in November.
When is the day?
Why it happened and
how it happened

Day in November
Sunsets are earlier.
Near to December
Feeling more squirrellier

Deer Season
November 24, 2019

Deer season is here.
Fills us with cheer..
All over there.
Better beware.

Wondering now.
Wondering how.
Feeling the wind.
Fills us with sin.

It's on a date.
Merciless fate.
Feeling the woods.
Just like it should.

Look at the deer.
Fills us with feer.
Bullets will fly.
Wondering why.

Don't you know now?
Feeling my brow
Don't let it waste.
Spray it with mace.

Great Dream
November 25, 2019

Radio playing that song again.
Playing that forgotten tune.
Song is sweet. So petite.
Should be over soon.

Maybe I'll just put it on rewind.
Just another forgotten tape.
Listening to Elton John.
And then I'll eat a crepe.

The music got that even beat.
That is just from the drums
And of course the guitar sound.
I see mice eating the crumbs.

Traveling across the miles.
To a wayward traveling inn.
Pull the guitar out of it's sack.
And play a forgotten hymn.

Waking up from this dream.
Opening up my eyes.
"Wow. Was that a great dream."
And I felt so wise.

Funny
November 26, 2019

Heavy. Heavy paper weights.
Sitting on the shelf.
Caring for other people.
Care about my self

Maybe we can get together.
Maybe we got style.
Trampling the grapes of wrath.
All in single file.

I got me a sense of humor.
Maybe it can feel.
Laughing on the riverside.
What a good steal.

Everybody laughs a lot.
Looking for a meal.
I am very hungry.
Dine behind the wheel.

Funny how the passing time.
Funny how it passed.
Funny how we set aside.
Going to the class.

Thanksgiving
November 27, 2019

A day before Thanksgiving.
She just looks so nice.
I Had to go and see her.
I had to just look twice.

She looked there so pretty.
She looked, oh, so hot.
Maybe she was incredible.
What a good spot.

Held her head high.
Marched off to bed.
What a good posture?
Wish I was dead.

Looking oh so pretty.
Looking oh so hot.
Did she ever look good.
What a good spot.

Man. I was wired.
Dismal I am soon.
Things are looking better.
By the last moon.

Toilet Seat
November 28, 2019

Dirty, dirty toilet bowl.
Ring around the collar.
Goes around like a
Dirty bottom dollar.

Greasy. Greasy goes around.
Like a 12-string guitar.
Playing all the strings like a
20-string sitar,

Poopoo undies everywhere.
And they realty smell.
Crappy, Crappy in your pants.
Another one just fell.

Flush it. Flush it everyone.
It goes down the toilet.
Flushing heaven down the drain.
High School's called LaFollette.

So when you come on home.
And you need a place to sit.
Just pull out your toilet seat.
And have a lit.

Slimeball
November 29, 2019

Slimeball
What you call
Anyone
six feet tall

Slimeball
Down you fall
Overhaul
Don't you stall

Slimeball
Cannon ball
Aerosol
and bean ball

Slimeball
an eyeball
Methanol
Montreal

Slimeball
Knuckleball
Butterball
alcohol

Last One
November 30, 2019

It's the last one.
It's the dirt.
It's the last one.
Don't it hurt?

It's the last one.
Dirt will fly.
It's the last one.
Makes me high.

It's the last one.
On the phone.
It's the last one.
Makes me moan.

It's the last one.
It's a fake.
It's the last one.
It's a milk shake.

It's the last one.
Make a start.
It's the last one.
You got a heart.

April 2020

Take It To The Bank
April 1, 2020

I took it to the bank.
And I went and drank.
And I want to thank.
And my heart sank.

And I ate a frank.
And I'm out of rank.
And I pulled a prank.
And my feet stank.

And I'm just a crank.
The train went clinkety-clank.
And I outrank.
That damn dirty Yank.

I just paid a franc.
Step across a plank.
Shot him point-blank.
On the gangplank.

Trying to be frank.
It's so dark and dank.
Move to Burbank.
I took it to the bank.

Suicide
April 2, 2020

Take a pill.
Suicide.
Make my will.
Suicide.

Go NA.
Suicide.
What I say.
Suicide.

Same old story.
Suicide
Defamatory.
Suicide.

Same old theory.
Suicide
Feeling weary.
Suicide

Live till end.
Suicide
How and when.
Suicide.

Hard Words
April 3, 2020

Releasing an album that made the charts.
Increments of movable clocks.
Increment pictures of wonderful art.
Monsters are coming from out of the loch.

Listening to pieces of my Mozart.
Traveling here and there to Bangkok.
Tracking out of here with a heart.
Tell her to put it into a sock.

This place was discovered by Descartes.
Wish that I went to Woodstock.
Sometimes wish I'm not that smart.
Pretty, pretty as a peacock.

Giving my car a good jump-start.
Up ahead is a roadblock.
That's what it's like driving a car.
When you're sent up you'll be wearing a smock.

Fell in love with the Prince of Denmark.
I am really a Czechoslovak.
Lost my virginity to Linda Starck.
So I have to pay for some stack.

Polyptch
April 4, 2020

Being famous, story says.
Being cool until you're dead.
Wonder if my horoscope
Means that I will be on dope.

And if I will be a liar.
Went to bed my pants n fire.
And I someday be awake.
OMG for goodness sake.

But to say that it's the end.
Is not worthy to be sent.
If your coats the color red.
Will I leave the newlywed.

As if I got so goddamn married.
I will say it just got scary.
It just means there's so many.
Polyptch and I go steady.

Then I see the United States.
Then I see the Watergate.
And we'll make it a holiday.
Being famous story says.

A Penny
April 5, 2020

Stink pink
Wanna mink
From a chink
Who is shrink

Going to the Marquee.
Going to drink some tea.
Going out with my bailee.
Going to Tennessee.

I admit my dad was bold.
I remember what was told.
It's my sexuality.
With my criminality.

I remember times I glazed.
And I left them in a haze.
I can say it in as a phrase.
Which is good nowadays.

I know my name is Kenny.
What if my name is Benny?
Certainly not me Jenny.
I wish I had a penny.

Doug Schwenn 76
April 6, 2020

Doug Schwenn 76.
Doag Swhwenn is the owner.
They fix brakes and mufflers there.
And he was a loner.

He was high school class as me.
We were the best of buddies.
We were in the same high school class.
Though I was a fuddy-duddy.

We went to Laughalot.
We had lots of good fun.
We were onto freshman ball.
Friends under the sun.

I remember playing center.
I also played linebacker,
We would rush in while the snap.
And we finally sacked her.

So someday we'll meet again.
Maybe at a class reunion.
Maybe so, we will go.
And have lots of fun. Yeah!

Pet Shop Boys
April 7, 2020

Pet Shop Boys a real gas.
"Don't want my
feelings restrained."
Don't want to blame.

Pet Shop Boys are my guess.
Want to talk sex.
Psychic ability
Make a hex.

"You don't see the writing
on the wall."
Don't know who
This may be.

Maybe I'll zonk out.
Then I'll go to sleep.
Wake up at one o'clock.
Paper comes at three.

I hear things this way.
One hundred BPM.
My psychic ability.
I'll be waiting to send.

Nightmare
April 8, 2020

Nightmare
I was bare
Truth or dare
Quite contraire.

Nightmare
Dreamt I got busted
In God I trusted
I'm maladjusted

Nightmare
Make me just scream
Feels like cream
In the word scream

Nightmare
I was under arrest
Her name was Mae West
I'm from Budapest.

Nightmare
The whose dam lot
Look for a spot
To make a plot

Georgian Bay
April 9, 2020

The way that I see it.
There's got to be a way.
I wonder where I'm going.
Move to Georgian Bay.

Got that stinking thinking.
We won't think the same.
Laughing at the problem.
Almost everyday.

Call it AC DC.
Anti Christ Devils Child.
Play that Rock 'n' Roll.
I say it with a smile.

I feel like I feel.
Feel like I'm weak.
Wished my name was Willie.
Right now as we speak.

Someday in the future.
Deep down in my soul.
We'll turn on the radio.
Play that rock 'n' roll.

Madonna
April 10, 2020

Madonna, Rock, paper, scissors.
What do you say? Really a winner.
Madonna. Got a lot a soul.
Looking good. Eat casserole.

Madonna. Look so good.
Turning heads in your childhood.
Madonna, Look so fine.
Read the headline.

Madonna. Sing real good.
She's invited to our neighborhood.
Madonna. Sing real sweet.
And her style is complete.

Madonna. I like her body.
And she gets kind of naughty.
Madonna. Is so great.
Full of love. Full of hate.

Madonna. Is so cute.
I'm in love. Can't compute.
Madonna. Is so hot.
I think I just hit the jackpot.

Pride
April 11, 2020

I'm your loyal friend.
I stay until the end.
Not on anybodies side.
I got my pride.

Lost my friend and kin.
Lost the place I'm lying in.
In a double homicide.
But I got my own pride.

My mother stole.
Case manager steels.
My girlfriend lied.
I got pride.

Hey. I did a striptease.
Wisconsin cheese style.
She's a sleaze.
But my own pride.

Don't fall out.
Jekyll and Hyde.
Pick a side.
But my pride.

Overdrawn?
April 12, 2020

Am I overdrawn?
That Is the question.
And if miso, piso?
What is the answer?

What is the answer?
Quite a dancer.
And I know.
Quite a prancer?

Am I overdrawn?
Go to the bank.
Looking for an answer.
Walk the gangplank.

There was a time.
When I as said.
I was overdrawn.
Then you'll call me dead.

They said, "Don't worry.
It's a natural thing.
Lots of people do it.
Overdrawing"

Weird Beard
April 13, 2020

I got a weird beard.
I wish I had a picture.
For you that is.
Putting it on thick.

My beard is so good.
It comes in handy.
It soaks up drool.
Like a bar of candy.

My beard is so great.
I like it that way.
I think it's cool.
On my birthday.

My beard is so line.
Pray for to keep.
I like it so much.
I use it to sweep. Ha. Ha.

My beard is so sweet.
It fits like a glove.
Makes me feel good.
When I make love.

Take Me Home Tonight
April 14, 2020

"Take me home tonight"
I think is so out-of-sight.
Could you give me a light.
And my name is Dwight.

"Take me home tonight."
You can guess my height.
Don't mean to be tight.
But I feel I'm right.

"Take me home tonight."
This is my delight.
I don't wanna fight.
I seen the limelight.

"Take me home tonight."
I am a socialite.
I have to indite.
I have to incite.

"Take me home tonight.:
You are ultra bright.
Cold out in the night.
Just go fly kite.

Zellweger
April 15, 2020

Zellweger. Zellweger.
How thee I love her.
I can just see her.
Like shes my sister.

How can I? How many?
Look into her.
I can see so much.
Yes indeed sir.

Don't make defense.
Into my mind.
Gives me a feeling.
Right down my spine.

Movie stars. Rock stars.
That's how I feel.
Seem so unfazed.
It was a steel.

Just me leading.
A life of crime.
Got sent to jail.
Just doing my time.

Saxophone
April 16, 2020

Kiss you is the issue.
Toilet tissue.
Don't be so meek.
Mozambique.

Take it to the mic
...no, no, no, no Mike.
What just happened
Here on planet Earth.

Triplicate.
Way to count them off.
You can't even cough.
You look so damn soft.

Featherbed.
That is the way to sleep.
I am in too deep.
Not trying to be cheap.

What I got is manners.
Like the city planners.
And the cheap paid fanner.
Get out your scanner.

Detective
April 17, 2020

Trying to be selective.
I am a detective.
I am against crime.
Because it's a crime.

Name is Detective Jackson.
Looking for some action.
Wonder how you feel.
Life behind the wheel.

I am really sorry.
Went on a safari.
Looking for a tiger.
Or a braunschweiger.

I feel so damn gray.
Looking for the NA way.
Because I feel clean.
But looking mighty mean.

What a holy wonder.
Lightning and the thunder.
Trying to be affective.
I am a detective.

Ding Dong Ditchit
April 18, 2020

Somebody been ringing my doorbell.
Wake me up in the middle of the night.
And there isn't any problem.
I think it's out-of-sight.

Somebody been ringing my doorbell.
Just someone to make fun.
Two o'clock in the morning.
And then my heart did spun.

Somebody been ringing my doorbell.
Please don't make an excuse.
Let's get out stuff together.
Couldn't we make a truce.

Somebody been ringing my doorbell.
Couldn't you just make a smile.
Wake me up in the middle of the night.
Smile like a crocodile.

Somebody been ringing my doorbell.
I really wanted a snooze.
Got things going on in the morning.
Because I got the blues.

Manic Reaction
April 19, 2020

Just having fun.
Under the sun.
Having a pun.
With my grandson.

Having a blast.
With my sportscast.
Making it last.
Doing it fast.

Doing it now.
With my eyebrow.
Pushing a plow.
Don't have a cow.

Making it when.
My name is Ken.
Pushing to send.
With my poor friend.

Oh OMG.
Painting a tree.
Give me the key.
Of my bungee.

KJ Blues
April 20, 2020

Don't wanna lose my cool.
A dirty game of pool.
I mean call the pocket.
I'm like in a rocket.

I am learning fast.
How to make it last.
Don't wanna lose these pants.
It will be a blast.

I make it sound so sweet.
Just like a piece of meat.
I feel like we're getting somewhere.
Just get out of my hair.

I got a major crush.
It got that kind of hush.
I swear and swear and swear.
I'm in my underwear.

I'm in my major place.
We met there face-to-face.
Oh god I'm in love.
With crap from above.

Top Of Page 292
April 21, 2020

I got stinkwood.
I got pleasure.
I got money.
I got treasure.

I got sainthood.
I got peace.
I got love
to say the least.

Let's draw swords.
I got friction.
What I got is
contradiction.

I got love.
I got hate.
What I got
that is my fate.

And the time comes.
Yes. My friend.
I will see you
in the end.

Eileen
April 22, 2020

Eileen, my cousin.
A dollar a dozen.
She really goes.
Under exposed.

She had the blues.
Her attitude.
She was in shipshape.
Look at the landscape.

She died of cancer.
She was a dancer.
She sure did socialized.
And did materialized.

I'll go to her wake.
With my handshake.
Hope I don't freak out.
Like Eagle Scout.

Tears made in heaven.
My lucky 7.
Eileen my cousin.
A dollar a dozen.

Aim It
April 23, 2020

Aim it high.
Aim it low.
Aim it fast.
Aim it slow.

Aim it left.
Aim it right.
Aim it far
Out of sight.

Aim it good.
Aim it bad.
Aim it happy.
Aim it sad.

Aim it wonderful.
Aim it sleezy.
Aim it hard.
Aim it easy.

Aim it all.
　　　(easy)
　　　　　(easy)
　　　　　　　(easy)

Bless This Mess
April 24, 2020

Bless this mess.
Cousin Eileen
I beg forgiveness.
Easy it seems.

She's the best person.
Ever comes around.
She makes those good cookies.
She makes not a sound.

She is so wonderful.
She is so neat.
Inheriting problems.
She is so sweet.

One of these days.
Incredible.
Find a cure for cancer.
Inedible.

State of the world.
Sure wore that hot dress.
COVID-19.
Bless this mess.